Moving To Florida

In **2021**

By:

James Hill

The Money Pro Series

D1309989

The Money Pro Series:

Save Thousands on Your Next New Vehicle

Save Thousands on Your Next Used Vehicle

Moving to Florida

Liar, Liar, Pants on Fire

Moving to Florida in 2021

TABLE OF CONTENTS

INTRODUCTION

Being over ten months into the covid-19 pandemic the state of Florida still has a raging problem, as do most states, with people catching and dying of the disease or problems related to it. Although the state has been very laxed on dealing with it, the infection rates and death counts are no different than states that have locked-down aggressively.

It is openly apparent that much of Florida's response has been due to political issues and pressures from business to maintain some degree of staying relevant, keeping the economy functioning. Only history will tell if this was the proper decision, an extremely difficult one to say the least. All we can do is to hope for our state leadership to make the best decisions for the residents of Florida and the guests who visit the state.

Now that being said, although the pandemic has changed some things hopefully on a temporary basis, in 2020 it is estimated that about 345,000 people has moved to Florida. That's 950 per day deciding to make a change to sunshine and paradise.

The state of Florida's primary economic driver is the tourist industry which has took a direct hit from the pandemic. For the first nine months of 2020, tourism **decreased** statewide by 28%, or from 99.8 million visitors in that same period in 2019 to 71.9 visitors in 2020.

According to state of Florida statistics, in 2019 Canadian travelers visiting Florida totaled about 3.6 million visitors. Two-thirds of the way through 2020, that number plummeted 99% to only about 36,000 guests.

No matter what events are taking place in the world, the warm breezes, shining sun, and gentile waves landing on the white sands of a pristine beach, are still the dreams of many who are looking for a piece of their paradise. For many, moving to the *Sunshine State* of Florida is the solution.

Having lived in Florida three times for over sixteen years, I've been able to experience what it takes for a successful move to the state. Hopefully I can share some insight on potential pitfalls of moving here and what to expect when you are living here.

As an adult, I moved back to Florida after being away from it for almost thirty-five years with the hopes and dreams of living in a place with all the accolades mentioned above of warm breezes and pristine beaches, along with all the other things you could expect in a tropical utopia. Each time after moving here the reality sets in that at times, *all isn't what it seems in paradise.*

Hurricanes, scammers, overcrowded conditions, mean people, crowded beaches, low paying work, beggars, etc. almost immediately puts a damper on the **Perfect Dream** of living in Florida.

Over the years, I've met hundreds of people and families who have moved to Florida, then after a few short years moved back to where they came from. They all come with great expectations and hopes, but after facing the reality of living day-to-day, those expectations were shattered and they find that the *grass isn't always greener* in paradise compared to where they originally came from. The major reasons for moving back to their original homes were economic, missed family and loved ones and for many older transplants, it gets too hot and muggy in the summer months.

This book isn't written to persuade you from not moving to your dream home or *your paradise*, but it is to enlighten on what to expect and the reality of such a major life changing move to the *Sunshine State*.

5

An old saying was that when a *flamingo* doesn't want to know what's going on around itself, they tend to bury their head in the sand to ignore what's happening. When moving to Florida, many people do this very same thing. They either ignore or just don't have the knowledge of what to really expect, with the hope that all will be good. After reading this book, this lack of knowledge doesn't have to be the case if you are planning on moving to Florida.

This book will give you the *reality* of what to expect if you decide to live in the paradise of Florida!

AMERICA'S TWENTY-SEVENTH STATE

I t was March 3rd, 1845 that Florida became a state. Since becoming a state, *Tallahassee* has been the capitol. The city of 196,667 people as of the latest count in 2019, makes it the ninth largest city in Florida. Tallahassee is located in the northern part of the state midway between *St. Augustine* (located on the Atlantic Ocean) and *Pensacola* (located in the western part of the panhandle on the Gulf of Mexico).

Although the estimated current population of Florida in mid-2020 is 21.99 million people, this wasn't the case when it became a state, or earlier when it was a territory in 1821. As a territory under Spanish rule, Florida was divided into two regions with the *Apalachicola River* as the boundary between the two.

East Florida's capital at that time was St. Augustine, while the capital of west Florida was Pensacola. Most people living in the territory which would eventually be called Florida at that time lived in the northern part of the state between and around these two capital cities.

In 1821, the current city of *Miami* didn't exist. The sparse population of that region was mostly made up of settlers from the Bahama's that migrated to the United States' mainland and homesteaded living areas for their individual families.

In these early territory days, *Key West* was owned by one man named *Juan Pablo Salas*. Salas was a Spanish naval officer stationed in St. Augustine. When America took possession of Florida, Salas eagerly sold it to an American.

The *Seminole Indians* also had various communities throughout the northern parts of the territory. The Seminole tribe was the largest native American Peoples in the area that would eventually become the state of Florida.

Before becoming a state, the *Legislative Council* met in Pensacola to decide on a capital that could be accessed easier by the representatives. At the time, it would take these council leaders from St. Augustine almost sixty days to make the trek of 400 miles to Pensacola.

All of Florida, including populated northern areas were nothing but undeveloped, thickly wooded terrain with unrelenting heat. Because of the distance of travel, the group of legislatures decided on finding a midway point to meet between St. Augustine and Pensacola.

The first capital was nothing more than a log cabin in Tallahassee, which was originally an *Apalachee Indian* settlement that had been abandoned.

When Florida became a state in 1845, a new, more permanent capital was completed on the same grounds of the log cabin. Over the next 105 years this capital went through many expansions and updates.

As the population of the state grew, more areas in central and southern Florida expanded with new cities. As growth occurred, there was talk of moving the capital to a more centralized area such as *Orlando*.

In 1967, a ground swell of support backed this move to Orlando, but was stymied when opponents worked diligently to expand the current complex in Tallahassee. They appropriated money to build a new capital complex with modern office buildings and facilities. This squashed the attempt to move the capitol.

As the city of Tallahassee grew in the 1970's, there was a push to tear down the old capital complex. Again, opponents worked to save this historic site and after much ado, the old capital complex was restored to the time frame of 1902. It is now a museum with artifacts, photos, memorabilia from Florida back to the days when it was a territory.

In 2020, the estimated population of the state is 21.99 million, up from the 2015 population of 20.3 million, and up 14.5% from the 2010 census of 18.8 million people.

The largest cities by population in 2020 are:

(Estimated before release of official 2020 census)

Jacksonville	926,371
Miami	486,388
Tampa	413,704
Orlando	291,739
St. Petersburg	271,842
Hialeah	243,208
Port St. Lucie	206,410
Cape Coral	199,503
Tallahassee	199,205
Fort Lauderdale	184,599
Pembroke Pines	177,058
Hollywood	158,239
Miramar	143,219
Coral Springs	137,007

Gainesville   134,205

There are ten other Florida cities that have a population between 100,000 and 120,000. These cities are: Lehigh Acres, Clearwater, Palm Bay, West Palm Beach, Lakeland, Pompano Beach, Miami Gardens, Brandon, Davie, Spring Hill and Boca Raton.

As with other large cities in the United States, Florida's cities are surrounded by smaller cities that make up the suburbs of that region. These suburbs included with the major city's population changes the order of the overall region's population.

Of the 67 counties in the state, the largest by population are:

Miami–Dade (*Miami*)	2,719,030
Broward (*Ft. Lauderdale*)	1,959,450
Palm Beach (*Palm Beach*)	1,510,660
Hillsborough (*Tampa*)	1,492,020
Orange (*Orlando*)	1,404,360
Pinellas (*St. Petersburg*)	976,934
Duval (*Jacksonville*)	966,858
Lee (*Ft. Myers*)	786,684
Polk (*Lakeland*)	742,957
Brevard (*Melbourne*)	608,681
Pasco (*New Port Ritchey*)	568,804
Volusia (*Daytona Beach*)	560,467

Over the past decades, Florida has dramatically changed its image from a retirement state with an older population and tourist destination to currently, still a tourist destination but with a younger overall geographic living here. Although, this change has been huge, the state still is a favorite place for retirees to live out their golden years.

In the past, agriculture was a major source of employment with citrus and cattle being major industries. Although agriculture still is a large part of Florida's economy, today, the tourism industry dominates the employment ranks with theme parks, beachfront resorts, the cruise industry and all the auxiliary industries and services that support tourism.

With a younger population, many families with children have created a need for more schools and higher institutes of learning. High-tech, modern schools are being built throughout the state to keep up with the population of school-aged children and young adults.

The oldest recognized institute of higher learning is *Rollins College* in *Winter Park*, which is near Orlando. It was organized in 1885 by *New England Congregationalist* who brought there liberal-arts type of education to the state.

With that being said, the *University of Florida (UF)*, currently in *Gainesville*, has its beginnings traced to 1853 when the *East Florida Seminary* acquired the *Kingsbury Academy* in *Ocala*. After the civil war it merged with the *Florida Agricultural College* in *Lake City*. The current university as we know today didn't form until 1906.

In 1947, when *University of Florida* started admitting women, there were only three state universities at the time, the other two were *Florida A&M*, and *Florida State College for Women*, which is now *Florida State University* in Tallahassee.

There are currently forty Universities, State Colleges and Junior Colleges in Florida. On top of that there are twenty-five religiously affiliated institutions, thirty-one technical/trade schools and forty-three private institutions.

Some of the best known are *University of Florida* (Gainesville), *Florida State University* (Tallahassee), and *University of Miami* (Coral Gables). In recent years with the younger population moving to Florida, *University of Central Florida* (Orlando), *University of South Florida* (Tampa) and *Florida International University* (Miami) have become growing institutions of higher learning in the state.

As with any large state in the United States, Florida has all the facilities and amenities you would want for a comfortable life. But unlike many older states in the north, because of the shift in population and age groups in recent years, many of Florida's facilities are newer and more modern, built more recently to keep up with the needs of a growing population.

The *state official marine mammal* is the lovable *Manatee.* Florida waterways are home to this slow-moving, adorable giant. Also called the *Sea Cow*, full-grown Manatees range from eight to fourteen feet in length and weigh one-ton. Female Manatees are larger than males. Life span is around thirty years, but some can reach forty years. Manatees give birth to a baby once a year.

Boaters are Manatees biggest predator. Hundreds of these mammals are injured or killed each year from careless boaters hitting them.

Blue Springs State Park in *Orange City* has a natural spring that is home to many of these docile creatures. Recently, on colder days, close to 500 Manatees have been counted near the springs. Visitors can rent canoes and float among these giant teddy-bears. Also, in summer months the park has a swimming area where at times a Manatee or two enters to socialize with humans.

If you are planning on a move to Florida in the future then you will become a part of the history of the sunshine state. It is estimated that by the year 2030, the population of Florida will reach 26 million. With such an increase, Florida will have to continue to build infrastructure and facilities to keep up with the needs of the people. This will only guarantee that Florida will have the state-of-the-art facilities for you and your family in the future.

DECIDING ON WHERE TO LIVE

Many people moving to Florida selects an area to live based on one of two major reasons. One, they know someone who currently lives in that area or two, they have visited the area in the past and just like it.

When I originally moved to the *Sunshine State*, my plans were to move to the *Naples* or possibly the *Fort Myers* area, which is in the southwest part of the state on the *Gulf of Mexico*. After spending two months travelling the coastline and spending several weeks in that area in a small motorhome, I changed my mind on where I wanted to live.

At the time the cost-of-living in that area was much higher compared to other coastal cities. Also, I visited during the winter months and the congestion from tourists and visiting snowbirds was crazy compared to other areas I had been to.

Although I could find a job in sales anywhere in the state, the affordability of a home, access to beaches and proximity to an airport were important to me.

Knowing someone in the area makes the move much easier than blindly going somewhere you know little about. If that isn't the case, then you need to do your homework or due-diligence before making the major decision on where to move. Learning and visiting about an area before relocating may save you a lot of sleepless nights later. Not only is it expensive to move and restart, but also you may end up in an area that won't be the hometown of your dreams.

Many newcomers to Florida have the dream of living near the *Atlantic Ocean* or the *Gulf of Mexico*. Some may find that it may be out of their financial budgets to accomplish this though. Generally, the closer to the coastlines that you live, the more expensive are homes and rentals. This factor forces many to move further inland where these costs can be less. This isn't always the case though. Inland living in certain areas or neighborhoods can be just as expensive as purchasing a home or renting near the ocean or gulf.

The ocean and gulf do offer the serenity of cool breezes, beautiful beaches and the sound of crashing waves. Though inland living doesn't offer these pleasures, Florida has 7,800 inland lakes that are an acre or more. This allows fantastic recreational opportunities 365 days a year with great weather throughout the state.

Florida's largest lake is in the southern part of the state and is named *Lake Okeechobee*. It is the fourth largest natural lake in the United States.

One item that you will not read about, but have to experience yourself is that the closer you get to a coastline, the cooler the summer temperatures are due to ocean and gulf breezes. Florida is considered tropical and is closer to earth's equator than any other part of the continental United States, so summer can be hot and humid. Again though, usually the closer you live to water, the more expensive it will be for housing.

There are a lot of rural areas in the state if you want to be living in more of a country atmosphere. Cattle, agriculture and horse farms are abundant throughout the state. According to the Florida *Department of Agriculture* statistics, in 2017 the state had 47,000 commercial farms. Orange and grapefruit production values represents more than 56 and 54 percent respectively of total United States production.

Also, Florida agriculture ranks first in crop values of cucumbers, squash, sugarcane, snap bean and tomatoes.

Although cattle and livestock production has slowed in recent years, Florida still ranks 18th in total cattle production in the U.S.

Normally, twenty to thirty miles from the coastlines you can live in a rural environment. The cost for housing will probably be less, unless you want to purchase a country-estate or several acres which is still going to sell at a premium price.

Florida's large cities are no different than any big city in the United States or Canada. Traffic jams, continual highway construction, new neighborhoods sprawling in every direction, and crime are daily annoyances. Because of the constant influx of new residents, cities and counties are always trying to keep up with growth.

The big difference between Florida's cities and one's in northern states, would be the beautiful weather to enjoy throughout the year with outdoor activities and festivals every week.

Other than the Orlando area and Tallahassee, Florida's major cities are near coastlines.

A big decision you will have to make after you decide the area to live is whether to purchase a home, condo, mobile home, multi-family unit or be a renter. If you have limited information concerning the area you plan on moving, the smartest thing to do is to rent for the first year.

Renting before purchasing will help you prevent making a large financial decision that you may regret in the future. According to 2020 statistics, there are 950-1,000 new people moving to Florida every day. Sounds like a lot, but there are plenty of rentals and plenty of room for growth in the state.

Purchasing a home immediately has many more costs involved than the home itself. Closing costs, repairs and updates add up fast. Also, homeowner's insurance can get expensive depending on the area you move. Not only will you have to carry regular homeowners' insurance, which will include wind/hurricane insurance, but most likely additional flood insurance too.

On numerous insurance information websites, Florida ranks second or third highest in regards to the yearly premium for homeowner's insurance. The average homeowner's insurance for the United States is around $1,200/year. Florida's average on one database says $1,900/year while a competing source says $3,500/year.

Up until a few years ago, no insurance company would insure a home or condo for any type of hurricane or wind damage. There was a state-sponsored program that allowed property owners to get this type of insurance. Today things have changed with insurance companies as they now bundle your regular homeowner's insurance with a wind/hurricane policy. From past experience, this has brought the overall cost of homeowner's coverage down.

Unfortunately, the location of your house may exempt you from the wind/hurricane coverage from a traditional insurance policy. If you live within 1500 feet of a major body of water, insurance companies don't have to provide wind/hurricane coverage. This is why the state-sponsored program named *Citizen's Insurance* is available for these homeowners. *Citizen's* is Florida's insurer of last resort, available if no other coverage is available.

If you must use this type of last-resort insurance option, its cost is generally more than a private insurer.

No matter if your wind/hurricane policy is with a private insurer or the state-sponsored program, the deductible is higher than normal homeowner's coverage. Hurricane deductibles typically are 2, 5 or 10 percent of the amount of insurance covering the dwelling at the time of the loss.

For more detailed information on this subject of Hurricane deductibles you can go to *MyFlorida.com* and direct yourself to the *Florida Department of Financial Services.*

If you are going to obtain a mortgage and the home is in a designated flood zone as depicted by the *Federal Emergency Management Agency (FEMA)*, you will be required to get flood insurance. This type of insurance can be purchased from the same company your homeowners is bought from. The average flood coverage cost is between $400–1,000 per year.

Before deciding on your move, contact a local Florida insurance agent in the vicinity where you want to live and they will be glad to assist you in an estimate of insurance rates for that area. Be sure to get a few quotes when you are ready to make that decision to purchase. On my current home, valued at $250,000, and two miles from the Atlantic Ocean, the quotes I had received went from $3,600/year with a company whom I was with for over forty-years to my current homeowners' insurance of $1,150/year.

Florida is primarily a peninsula with a panhandle in the most western part of the state. The highest point in Florida is 345 feet above sea-level. *Briton Hill*, which is in the western panhandle region just south of the Alabama state line holds this honor of highest point in the state.

The peninsula part of the state only averages about 30 feet above sea-level. Orlando, in the middle of the state is 82 feet above sea-level while Miami is only 6 foot above sea-level.

As climate change continues to melt glaciers in the *Artic* and *Antarctica* regions, rising sea levels make coastline properties at risks of flooding. Coastal regions aren't the only places with potential flooding, inland areas near lakes, rivers, streams and water retention areas may have flooding problems under the right circumstances.

According to *Ben Strauss* from an article in the *Miami Herald*, *"Florida is in the crosshairs of climate change. Rising seas, a population crowded along the coast, porous bedrock, and a relatively common occurrence of tropical storms put more real estate and people at risk from storm surges aggravated by sea level rise in Florida, than any other state by far."*

Miami is already having issues with major roads flooding almost daily because of high and low tides that are a natural part of nature. It is predicted that if the current rise in sea levels continue, in the next seventy-five years oceans will rise 11-13 feet. The altitude of Miami is only six feet above sea-level which will result in the city disappearing underwater unless walls, dykes, barriers, etc. are built to hold back the water.

Without planning and action Florida is predicted to be under water by the next millennium. If you are young and planning to live a lifetime near the coastal regions, or if retired and planning on leaving your coastal estate to family take into consideration that the home may be under water in the future.

If you plan on renting a home, apartment, or condo you will have to pass the scrutiny of credit checks and criminal background checks. This also may occur if you plan on purchasing a residence covered by a *Homeowners Association (HOA)*. The cost involved for these checks are normally an expense that you will have to pay ranging from about $35 to $125.

Throughout Florida, affordable rental housing is becoming a greater and greater issue. In the past decade, many older apartment complexes have been purchased by developers and converted into condominiums that are sold as single-family units. This has shrunk the established apartment market. Because of this, it has caused the rents to rise substantially making housing unaffordable to many lower income people and families.

In many areas of Florida there is a building boom of modern, new apartment complexes which helps alleviate the shortage of rentals. Unfortunately, rental rates in these newly established communities are substantially higher.

According to *Apartments.com*, the average rental costs in 2020 for a two-bedroom apartment in the following cities are:

Orlando	$1,376/month
Miami	$1,710/month
Jacksonville	$1,291/month
Tampa	$1,444/month
Cape Coral	$1,368/month
Ft. Lauderdale	$2,117/month
Lakeland	$1,157/month
Palm Bay	$1,066/month
Ocala	$1,010/month
Melbourne	$1,438/month
Port Orange	$1,290/month

Palm Coast	$1,163/month
Key West	$2,323/month
Sarasota	$1,498/month
Destin	$1,652/month
West Palm Bch	$1,237/month

Purchasing a home in Florida is the dream of many, especially retirees who have worked a lifetime for the opportunity to live the good life in the sunshine state. The good news is that purchasing a home in Florida is much more affordable than many other states.

Florida ranks #24 in the cost of purchasing a home compared to other states. In June 2020, the *National Association of Realtors* statistics stated that the average cost of a home in the United States was $295,300. In July 2020, the average cost of a Florida home was $270,000 according to the *Florida Association of Realtors. Zillow* has the average cost at about $255,000.

A median average of a top tier home in Florida was $432,633, single family home $266,350, bottom tier single family $158,180 and condo $194,264.

Florida has many mobile homes since they are much more affordable for many people than purchasing a stick or block-built home. Most mobile homes are in parks with amenities such as pools, clubhouses, pathways, game rooms, exercise facilities, dog parks, etc. Although Florida has over 830,000 mobile homes, compared to the other forty-nine states, they still only rank #17 in percentage of mobile homes compared to overall housing.

Although the initial cost of a mobile home can start at $150,000 in some cases, generally the cost of purchasing a pre-owned one is much less starting around $25,000. Beware though, the overall cost in the long-run of a mobile home in a park will be much more than your original cost to purchase.

Mobile home lot rent can be as inexpensive as $300-400 a month, but may run as much as $1,000+ a month with yearly increases. If you are paying that much plus the cost of the mobile home of $20,000-150,000, then it may be wiser financially to pay a mortgage on a stick or block-built home, not a mobile home.

Another consideration before purchasing a mobile home is that they can easily be damaged when a tropical storm or severe winds hit. Florida is prone to tropical storms and hurricanes every year. Unlike a tornado that destroys a path a few miles long, a hurricane can wipe out a third of the state from the Gulf of Mexico to the Atlantic Ocean with no problem.

When purchasing any type of property to live, mobile home, condo, single-family home etc., you will probably have a *Homeowners Association (HOA)*. These are common in Florida communities. HOA's normally have a book-of-rules and regulations you must abide by to live in that neighborhood or community. Besides that, you will have a monthly or yearly fee that pays to enforce the rules, keep common areas cleaned, and periodically keep residents updated on neighborhood issues.

HOA fees can be as little as $150 per year or as much as $4800 per year. Before deciding on a place to live be sure that you ask and understand the HOA fee involved. Also, if possible, ask to see the community rule book that you are expected to live by.

Coming from the north and never having to deal with an HOA, the rules and regulations seemed crazy when I first read and experienced them. Things as no pets, no fencing or certain types of fencing, no cars parked in driveway overnight, no fruit trees in yard, no gardens, only certain plants around home, etc. seemed to be an infringement on my rights of purchasing a $250,000 home, but these rules are enforced and you can be fined or lose your property with multiple violations.

HOA's are meant to keep the quality of neighborhoods up and they do that, but sometimes they can go a little overboard with tedious rules and dumb regulations.

With a lot of retirees living in Florida who no longer work or only have minimal things to do, many bide their time complaining and thinking up rules for their HOA's. With that in mind, a lot of retired neighbors are extremely nosy and constantly in your business. Now this could happen anywhere but because of the high concentration of retirees living here, it is worse than most other areas of the United States.

If you move to a home without an HOA, other problems can arise that most people wouldn't consider. Although, in recent years this has become less of a problem, it still exists where a mobile home is put up next to a $500,000 home. Or your neighbor has derelict vehicles rusting away in the yard. How about a twenty-year old refrigerator sitting on the front porch permanently next to your new home?

When hearing things like that, the HOA looks much better, but still you must put up with the grinding rules that may accompany some of them.

Property taxes in Florida are very reasonable compared to many states. In owner-occupied homes, the effective tax rate is ranked 26th compared to other states. If you live in the property you can **homestead** it, which gives you a major discount on your property taxes. Also, if you are a senior or on disability you can get reductions on property taxes.

If you plan on using the home as an investment or be a part-time resident, then you will pay quite a bit more for property taxes. As an example, a home of an acquaintance is homesteaded but the next door neighbors is not. The neighbor's property tax is thirty-two percent higher than the owner-occupied one.

On the homesteaded $240,000 property the tax is $2,600, while the neighbor's non-homesteaded property tax is $3,800/year.

Here are a few more items to keep in mind when looking for a home to live.

Sinkholes are a problem in Florida. The soil is a porous limestone and erodes easily, so underground washouts (sinkholes) can occur anywhere.

This for most will not be a problem if you rent or purchase a home in a neighborhood already established or being newly built. Although a sinkhole has appeared near newer structures. Homebuilding companies take extra effort on making sure homes are on solid ground with the least chance of having a sinkhole problem.

Most homeowner's insurances won't cover sinkhole damage to your home so be aware that this could be a problem. I would never suggest not to move to Florida just because of the sinkhole problem. The odds are slim that you could be affected, but take note that this is an issue that most other states don't have.

If you are accustomed to a home with a basement, sorry to say that basements are almost non-existent in Florida. This is because the ground-water table won't allow for a basement without flooding it out.

Since Florida has a tropical climate year-round, *termites* live and breed easily. Wood frame houses and roof rafters are prone to damage from them. Before purchasing a home, a termite inspection will be needed. Then, after your purchase, professional treatment with yearly inspections is recommended.

Another concern when determining on where to live is that of wildlife. *Alligators, bears* and *birds-of-prey* are everywhere. If you live near inland water such as a pond, lake, or drainage canal, be aware that your pets may be in danger of disappearing. Also, even when a pet is in your presence an alligator will still attack and you could be a victim also.

Bears are common everywhere, even in larger cities. They root through trash, barbeque pits, etc. at night forging for food. Bear attacks on pets and humans are not common since they want to avoid people.

Birds-of-Prey are also abundant. Small animals and pets are perfect meals for many of these birds. Rabbits are very scarce in Florida, matter of fact I didn't see one in twelve years because of the birds-of-prey and other predators.

Love Bugs are a nuisance Floridians get accustomed to normally twice a year. *Love Bugs* attach to each other and fly in swarms in late April-May and again in late August-September. Four to five weeks, twice a year they appear and cover doors, cars, etc.

Love Bugs don't bite or sting and are relatively harmless except for flying all around you. They do cause damage to automobile paint when they are squashed on the front of the vehicle from driving. Dead ones on a vehicle for a day or two can ruin a cars clearcoat so be ready on a daily basis to wash them off.

If you live within a few miles of the coastlines, another problem you will have is the rusting of anything metal you own. I've seen four-year old cars rusted around the window frames and wheel-wells that had sat outside near the ocean. Refrigerators, stoves, metal window frames, metal doors, hinges, etc. are prone to rusting the closer you live to the coastlines. Sea-mist and fogs close to the ocean are filled with salt particles that tend to make things deteriorate more quickly.

A casualty of this rusting problem is the chrome on vehicles and motorcycles. Even garaged, the issue of rust forming can be a problem.

All the above are things most people wouldn't consider when moving to paradise, but they effect everyday life when you live here. After you're here for a period of time you will get used to these nuisances, among other things that you would never had expected before moving here.

After a while it all becomes tolerable, especially when the temperature up north is twenty-degrees with a windchill of zero and a foot of snow expected. You'll be sitting here with a low of sixty-five degrees and a daytime temperature of eighty!

JOBS, WORK & INCOME

During the post-recession economy after 2008, Florida, like most states, has enjoyed a steady gain of employment which has resulted in low unemployment rates and an increase in average income. Then came March 2020 and the Covid-19 crisis.

Although in November 2019 Florida showed a 3.6% rate of unemployment, it rose to a high of about 14.5% in May 2020. This rate was high but not as severe as many other states such as Nevada which was over 25%.

At the end of 2020 the unemployment rate has remained steady at about 6.4%. Like many states during the early days of the pandemic, Florida literally closed down except for crucial, essential businesses. After the initial lockdown, Florida's *Governor DeSantis* aggressively reopened business with some restrictions but loosely enforced. At the end of 2020, some restrictions are still in place but are mainly ignored with no retribution. Many local jurisdictions do have more stringent restrictions, but overall covid-19 is mainly ignored.

In the past, Florida was known for low-wages and predominantly a tourism/service economy that supported the reason for low pay. Up until 2019, Florida's minimum wage was the national rate of $7.25/hour.

In 2018, Florida voters passed that the wage in Florida would become $15.00 over a period of time. In 2019, it went up to $8.46/hour. On January 1, 2021, it will be raised to $8.65/hour and another increase in September 2021 to $10.00/hour.

These increases will continue through the year 2026 which will top out at $15.00/hour.

According to the Census Bureau, in 2019 median household income in Florida is reported to be $59,227 per year and the per capita income was $31,619. In comparison, the median household income in the United States is $62,843.

In 2019, there were thirty-two states (including D.C.) with a higher median household income than Florida, with the highest being District of Columbia at $92,266. Five states including Maryland, New Jersey, Massachusetts, California and Hawaii are all over $80,000/year. The lowest medians are Mississippi, Arkansas and West Virginia which are all below $50,000/year.

Income inequality in the past has been a major issue in Florida with some people making huge amounts of money, while a majority struggled at the bottom of the income scale. This trend has been changing due to more younger people moving into the state with families and increased higher education which results in higher paying jobs.

Because of an aging population and so many people on government programs such as Medicare/Medicaid, there are a great number of jobs in the medical fields that pay well above the state average income, although still below the national average for those occupations. Also, the state has an overabundance of attorneys and their staffs which earn better than average incomes. Once you move to Florida you will be bombarded daily with television ads, billboards, radio advertising, etc. with attorney ads ready to take your case and sue any infraction against you.

You have to remember when moving to Florida, much of the population came here to retire with a set income for life. Most retirees don't work or only want part-time jobs because they have pensions, retirement income or social security. They bring their own money and don't have to rely on a large income from a job. This hurts the overall job market in two ways: First, with a set income, retirees want to keep their cost-of-living as low as possible so they don't go out and spend money. People with a set income want a cheap meal, inexpensive things to do and so on. For a business to survive they must keep labor costs down, keeping salaries low since these costs are normally their biggest expenses. Second, most retirees in there early years of retirement need something to do or additional income so they work part-time jobs at a wage less than most people would normally expect.

If a retiree will work for 70% of the pay in a job, then that takes the job away from a person trying to make a living to raise a family.

Here are a few examples of how Florida's wages differ from some other areas of the country. These are based on personal friendships and experiences:

A union electrician of twenty-two years making $76,000+ a year moved to Florida with his family which included two teenagers still living at home. With a superb work resume he thought it would be easy to get a job and live the *good life*. After applying for a dozen jobs, which all tried to hire him at less than half his past wage he took one that paid about sixty-percent of what he previously made. After a year of getting deeper and deeper in debt moved back north to financially recover from the mistake of moving here.

A 38-year-old teacher that was making $48,000 per year moved to Jacksonville with her family. After working for the first year as a substitute teacher for $12.00 per hour finally got a full-time educator's job at $29,500 per year. Only lasted another school year before having to go back to where she originally moved from.

A professional automobile dealership manager from New Jersey making $100,000+ per year moved to the Daytona area but couldn't find a managerial job so he took a salespersons position selling cars. The job was commission only, three days off per month, which he was berated when he took a day off, worked twelve hours a day and made $43,000-$55,000 per year. After doing this for four years went back to where he came from.

A roofer from Virginia making $22.00 per hour moved to the Melbourne area with his wife and three children. After looking for a decent paying job, ended up taking a $11.50 roofing job with no benefits. After a summer of working on roofs that approached 110 degrees daily, he packed the family up and moved back to Virginia.

After hearing the above, you may be thinking, well the cost-of-living is cheaper in Florida so you can live on less, or since Florida doesn't have a state income tax, making less is okay.

To debunk those two ideas, the cost-of living is no different than other states. Gasoline, housing, property tax, food, medical are all in line with other states. On top of that auto insurance in Florida is the third most expensive of the fifty states because it is a *no-fault* insurance state which has approximately one in four drivers having no insurance which raises the costs for everyone. Also, with an older population driving, seniors are more prone to accidents which also increases insurance companies' pay-outs and expenses that are passed along to you in premiums.

As to having no state income tax, that is correct. Most states have an income tax ranging from 3% to 7%. Living in Florida and working, the state average $31,619 per capita income, a person will save $948-$2,213 in taxes over other states with an income tax. Depending on your driving record, the savings in taxes can easily be offset by the higher insurance cost for automobile insurance.

Larger cities do have a more stable economy that is diversified from the tourism economy that dominates the state. Cities such as Jacksonville, Tampa, Tallahassee and Miami have national and regional companies in insurance and banking which tend to be better paying jobs.

Florida is a *right-to-work* state. Generally, a right to work state means wages are lower than states that are **not** *right-to-work*. This holds true in Florida. With an abundance of people fighting for every job possible and being a *right-to-work* state, these things tend to keep wages lower.

Unions are fairly rare to find in Florida. Some federal jobs are unionized such as workers at the *Kennedy Space Center*, and numerous military facilities in the state. But other than that, very few higher paying union occupations are available. Again, this is due to Florida being a *right-to-work* state.

Florida is not a large manufacturing state. Although over the past few years more companies have moved here, manufacturing is still a small part of the overall job market. Many jobs that are available in manufacturing are manpowered by *Temp-Agencies*. These Temp-Agencies are like employment offices that supply personnel to business, as you are considered an independent contractor. Working through a temp-agency you receive no benefits or perks. You work for your wage and that's it. Many people find work this way making $10-14.00 per hour working in factories producing everything from car parts to suntan lotions.

Just looking through a few newspapers and job boards today, about 90 percent of the ads are looking for telemarketers, door-to-door salespeople or commissioned sales jobs. This is common. Also, a job that has caught my eye is for a part-time firefighter. The job requires the applicant to have firefighter and EMT certification. The job pays $12.00 per hour with no benefits from the city.

If you are moving to Florida and must depend on a good income to survive or raise a family then keep in mind that higher paying jobs are more difficult to find than many other areas of the country. If you are living pay check to pay check with minimal backup funds then find a job here before you move.

If you are a retiree and plan on just living off your current pension and assets and they are limited, it gets boring sitting around day and night staying home attempting to conserve your money. The reality is that there are only so much beach or theme parks you can do. You might want to get part-time employment to keep busy or supplement your income. If this is you, then Florida is a great place to be with beautiful weather and lots of recreational things to do.

Many retirees say, *'sitting around daily not only gets boring but also becomes expensive'*!   I can vouch for that as I've also have tried to totally retire. After so much television, exercising, washing the car, mowing the grass, etc. you get bored and end up going out day after day eating, drinking and spending money. Before you know it, a year has come and gone and you've spent the money budgeted for the next two years.

Myself, like so many others who has good work ethics, a lot of knowledge in their fields, and the thought that I could make it anywhere, moving to Florida was a total shock when it came to work and income. After reading this, you have been warned, so be prepared if you plan on working when you move.

As with anything in life, there are usually good and bad. Although I've listed some of the potential pitfalls above; the sun, surf and living in paradise can easily outweigh the negatives of living in Florida.

DAILY LIFE AS A FLORIDIAN

I'm going to break this chapter down into two distinct areas. It'll talk about daily life as a full-time worker, then as a part-time worker which will include not working, but living more of a retirement lifestyle.

If you work full-time and depend on the income you make to live, then chances are your daily life will not be much different than what you are experiencing now. You get up early, eat breakfast, send kids to school, go to work, make dinner after work, watch television and go to bed.

Depending on the school district, the starting times of schools vary greatly. In some areas school busses are picking children up at 6 a.m. and school lets out around 2 p.m. In other areas, school doesn't get started until 7:30 a.m. and school busses are still running around with kids until 5:30-6:00 p.m.

If you are involved with the service or tourism industry, many employees start very early getting tourist ready for a day of fun. Other jobs not in these industries are probably more normalized hours starting at 8:30-9:00 a.m.

Living in a larger city, you still have traffic congestion and continual road construction which is no different than most major cities. Commuting is also very common in Florida since better paying jobs are minimal in some areas. It is not uncommon for someone to drive an hour or more each way to work. I have worked in the past with people who drove over an hour-and-a-half each way while working a twelve-hour day.

If earning an income is critical after you move here it is important to research job opportunities available in the area you

34

may want to live before committing to a particular area. Also, if you move here spontaneously and purchase a home, then find out theirs no work locally that fits your needs, you will be one of those driving hours a day to and from work.

If picturesque sunrises or sunsets are important to you then deciding on which coast line you may want to live will be important. If you're into sunrises, then the eastern coastline of Florida is where you want to be. The new day appears from behind the ocean and rises in the sky in brilliant fashion.

If sunsets are what you desire, then living on the west coast or the panhandle regions are where you would want to consider moving. Nothing is more comforting than watching a beautiful sunset as our gigantic sun disappears over the edge of the earth as though the Gulf of Mexico is devouring it.

Want the best of both worlds? Then south of Miami in the *Florida Keys* is the spot. With the narrow keys you can enjoy the morning sunrise then about fourteen hours later go across the street and watch the sunset.

On days off there is always plenty to do. The good things about moving to Florida in regards to recreational activities are that every weekend something will be going on such as street parties, festivals, events, fairs, and much more. If you live near the coasts you always have the beach which is a free venue to visit and have fun. Beware though, that on a nice day beaches get very crowded and many locals tend to avoid it after the newness wears off.

After living here for a few years many people don't go to the beach more than once a year. The first few years of living here the beach is new and exciting. After years of fighting the crowds, burnt skin, sand in the car, many get tired of it and don't go anymore.

I tend to relate this not going to the beach with, if your favorite dessert in the world was German chocolate cake and you could eat it every day of your life, eventually you'd get sick of it and stop eating it. Going to the beach, if you live close to it, tends to evolve the same way.

In a limited number of coastal towns, driving on the sand at the beach is still allowed. Although over the years this has ended in many areas, some counties still allow it. For a small fee, you can take your vehicle onto the sand and park for the day, or drive the length of the beach enjoying the sights and sounds of the ocean.

Here are the counties and cities that still allow beach driving:

Amelia Island/*Nassau County*

Daytona Beach/*Volusia County*

Huguenot Park/*Duval County*

New Smyrna Beach/*Volusia County*

St. Augustine Beach/*St. Johns County*

Grayton Beach/*Walton County* *(limited to 150 permits/year))*

Believe it or not there are some hazards of driving the beach. Each year several people gets hit or ran over as they are sunbathing or just not paying attention. This is the primary reason that beach driving has been eliminated on several beaches in the state over the past thirty years.

If you do plan on taking your vehicle on the beach, a problem that you will encounter is an invisible one. It is that the fine grains of sand get into all mechanical areas of your car such as brakes, engine areas, fan belts, air conditioning systems, etc. and tend to wear these parts down prematurely. The grit from the sand becomes like sandpaper as it grinds down movable parts of a vehicle. Although this can be a major problem if you drive often on the beach, the excitement and pleasure from the drive is hard to resist.

Something not unique to Florida, but very prevalent are the number of homeless, beggars and panhandlers you see daily. Because of year-round good weather, not only the working and retirees flock to Florida, but also the homeless and people who don't want to work or have life-issues such as drug, alcohol addictions or mental health issues. Many major street intersections have people holding signs asking for money, for some it's a full-time job. Sleeping on park benches, under piers, bus stops and public areas is something you will get used to because it's everywhere.

Many towns are starting to address this issue by building homeless shelters to help get people off the streets. Also, new laws are popping up throughout the state that limits or eliminates begging and panhandling in their municipalities.

With all the homeless and panhandlers, they don't account for much of the crime towards others. Very seldom will you hear about a homeless person committing crime against another person. Now you will hear about a small portion of them stealing and getting caught, but it doesn't seem to be a major problem. Many times, the stealing has to do with drug addictions.

Outdoor activities, other than the beach are plentiful throughout Florida. Golf is inexpensive and can be played 365 days a year. If theme parks are your thing, then as a Florida resident most of them have big discounts for you.

The same thing with cruises out of the five major cruise seaports in Florida at *Jacksonville, Port Canaveral, Ft. Lauderdale, Miami* and *Tampa*. For panhandle residents, *Mobile, Alabama* also has a seaport for cruises. Florida residents can enjoy major savings and on top of that, if you are flexible, you can get *last-minute* cruises saving as much as 80%.

The covid-19 pandemic has greatly affected many activities that Floridians have taken-for-granted. As of March 2020, cruises have been cancelled until further notice. Although it is estimated that cruising will begin again in the Summer 2021, this starting date has come-and-gone multiple times in the past year.

Theme parks are open but are limiting capacity. Mask-wearing, social distancing, etc. are recommended. Crowds are much smaller than in the past since incoming tourists has dramatically decreased due to Covid-19. Unlike theme parks in the state of California being still closed almost a year since the start of covid-19, Florida's theme parks were only closed for approximately three-months.

Boating is a big pastime for many Florida residents. With so much water available, weekends bring out tens-of-thousands of boating enthusiasts.

If you don't have the storage area to purchase a boat, there are *time-share boat clubs* that with a membership fee will allow for you to use different types of boats throughout the year without the expense of owning it.

Anywhere you go that has water involved you will see fishermen and women throwing their lines out. When fishing in Florida you will be required to have a fishing license. The fee structure is different for a resident than a visitor. There are also several various types of licenses that can be purchased. The two most common are for freshwater or saltwater.

Sport and deep-sea fishing are popular since theirs a gigantic ocean and gulf that surrounds the state. Besides private charters, group charters go out daily taking up to fifty people at a time for a half-day or full-day of fishing. This is very popular with tourists who don't have the pleasure of doing this in their hometown areas.

Surfing has a prominent place around the coastlines of Florida. Although you won't see a lot of senior citizens on the waves, you will see dozens of people in all age groups on their boards navigating the swells.

The world-famous *Ron Jon Surf Shop* in *Cocoa Beach* is a must see if you are on the east coast of Florida. If lucky, hometown hero and six-time *World Champion* surfer **Kelly Slater** will be around the shop or on the beach when you visit.

The city of *New Smyrna Beach* holds the honor of the *Shark-bite Capital of the World!* Thankfully, most shark-bites don't kill the victim, but a chunk of skin taken from a leg, arm or anywhere on the body results in a painful and unforgettable experience.

Paddle boarding has become popular over the past fifteen years. This is a type of surf board that is between 12-17 foot long that you either kneel or stand and use an oar to guide yourself on the ocean or waterway. It not only takes balance, but also upper body endurance which makes this good exercise besides being fun.

Florida is blessed with having eleven *National Parks*. These areas of serenity and beauty are throughout the state. Here is a list of them and the areas that they are in:

Big Cyprus National Preserve *(Ochopee)*

Biscayne National Park *(Miami, Key Biscayne, Homestead)*

Canaveral National Seashore *(Titusville, New Smyrna Beach)*

Castillo de San Marcos National Monument (*St. Augustine*)

De Soto National Memorial (*Bradenton*)

Dry Tortugas National Park (*Key West*)

Everglades National Park (*Miami, Naples, Homestead*)

Ft. Caroline National Memorial (*Jacksonville*)

Ft. Matanzas National Monument (*St. Augustine*)

Gulf Islands National Seashore (*Gulf Breeze*)

Timucuan Historic Preserve (*Jacksonville*)

Besides the parks listed above, Florida also has 175 nature reserves, recreation areas and historic sites that are managed by the state for recreation and preserving the history of the state. Several of these parks were once privately owned as tourist attractions. Over the years the state has purchased or were donated these sites to become a part of the *Florida State Park* system.

According to the *WorldAtlas.com*, Florida's coastline is 1,350 miles on the *Atlantic Ocean* and *Gulf of Mexico*. Because of these many miles, lighthouses were a major safety precaution to assist merchant and pleasure ships since before the incorporation of the state.

Forty-nine lighthouses have toasted Florida's coastline over the years. Twenty-nine of them are still operational or has been made into historic sites. Fourteen conduct public tours and six have grounds that can be toured.

If you enjoy a little more sedentary fun, then several Florida beaches are known for a variety of colorful, elegant *shells*! Many beaches are just sand or chips of shells, but these thirteen locations are loaded with *shells* that make great souvenirs of your visit to the beach. Keep in mind, it is illegal to take a *live shell* from the beach.

Amelia Island	Hutchinson Island	Navarre Beach
Shell Island	Honeymoon Island	Sand Key Park
Ft. De Soto Park	Venice Beach	Ft. Myers Beach
Marco Island	Barefoot Beach	Anna Maria Island
	Sanibel/Captiva Island	

Sanibel/Captiva Island is near Fort Myers on Florida's west coast. This beautiful beach is considered *'The Shelling Capital of the World'*! *Venice Beach* located also on the west coast is known as *'The Shark Tooth Capital of the World'*!

Florida has several professional sports franchises in major cities. These include, Major League Baseball (MLB), National Basketball Association (NBA), National Hockey League (NHL), National Football League (NFL), Professional Soccer (American Association Football Club) and National Women's Soccer League.

MLB spring training comes to Florida each March, then the season continues with the *Florida State League* which is comprised of ten minor league clubs throughout the state. Here are the teams and the professional club they represent:

Bradenton Marauders (Pirates)	Dunedin Blue Jays (Blue Jays)
Clearwater Threshers (Phillies)	Daytona Tortugas (Reds)
Lakeland Flying Tigers (Tigers)	Tampa Tarpons (Yankees)
Ft. Myers Mighty Mussels (Twins)	Jupiter Marlins (Marlins)
Palm Beach Cardinals (Cardinals)	St. Lucie Mets (Mets)

Since 1968, *The Kennedy Space Center (KSC)* located on Florida's east coast near the cities of *Titusville* and *Cocoa Beach* has been

America's primary launch center for manned and unmanned rockets. The center is managed by the *National Aeronautical and Space Administration (NASA)*.

A new generation of space travel has developed in the past few years with *SpaceX*. The company owned by **Elon Musk**, who also owns the car manufacturer *Tesla*, has formed a union with *NASA* to launch and support space travel and exploration by a private company. *SpaceX* will launch dozens of rockets in the year 2021, which brings hundreds-of-thousands of people to the region for the extravaganza.

KSC is a major tourist destination with tours, museums, one-on-ones with astronauts and unbelievable rocket launches. Space launches can be observed throughout central Florida and is a true spectacle that everyone needs to experience. Many locals look forward to launch days and make it a planned outing to see these history making events.

The gambling industry has grown in Florida over the past fifteen years. Two major casinos in the state are the *Seminole Hard Rock* located in *Hollywood* and *Ybor City (Tampa)*.

Around the state are located some smaller casinos that offer limited gaming. Unlike major casino hubs like *Las Vegas*, *Atlantic City* and *Biloxi*, Florida's laws on casinos are much stricter. Games such as *craps* is only limited to *virtual* play. All casinos don't offer live *blackjack*. Many just offer *slots, virtual blackjack, roulette* and *baccarat*.

Some of the best gambling for Vegas style gambling are offered on daily *casino cruise excursions*! These depart from various coastal cities and take patrons out once or twice a day, five or six miles into the ocean to gamble. These cruises do offer live blackjack and craps. Some are free admission while others have a minimal boarding fee. These cruises lasts five to seven hours each trip.

Greyhound dog racing once had 25 tracks in Florida but as of January 1, 2021, none remains. In 2018, voters decided that greyhound racing was cruel to the animals and voted it eliminated by constitutional vote. Most of these tracks also had *poker rooms* that have been expanded since the vote in 2018.

Pari-mutual betting on horses is allowed in Florida with several facilities throughout the state. *Gulfstream Park* (Hallandale Beach), *Hialeah Park* (Hialeah) and *Tampa Bay Downs* are three of the top thoroughbred tracks in the United States.

Many former greyhound tracks, poker rooms and current horse tracks offer *simulcast wagering* where you can go, watch horse and dog racing, harness racing and Jai-Alai matches from throughout the world and place wagers. Most counties have at least one *simulcast wagering* facility.

Florida poker rooms offer many live games such as Texas Hold-em, Omaha, and Stud Poker. Most poker facilities are open early and stay open into the wee-morning and on weekends there is twenty-four-hour action. Many Poker Rooms are now offering some casino type card games such as one card poker, three card poker, Caribbean poker, Pai Gow Poker, and Bonus Poker.

Night life varies greatly throughout the state. Seniors and retirees usually start the evening at around 4-5 p.m. going out for early-bird specials and happy-hour drinks. The next wave starts at 6-8 p.m. with the tourist going out for dinner and nutrition after a busy day. Then starting at 9-10 p.m., younger people or some tourists who has energy remaining from the current day, will start clubbing or hit the dance venues.

Although dance and night-clubs are in all areas, the coastal towns and Orlando are the hot spots. Many of these areas such as *South Beach (SoBe)* in Miami offer a vibrant nightlife with all night partying, dancing and entertainment.

What's a classy night out in Florida? Unlike most major night life areas like Chicago, New York City, Los Angeles, the attire for a night out in Florida is a sun dress or shorts for women, and shorts, sandals and a polo type shirt for men. Dressing-up is uncommon, you just don't see a lot of it except for the very hip areas.

Florida is known by motorcyclist as one of the top places to ride in the United States. Several cities have events that range from 3 days to two-weeks in length. Here are some of the larger events:

Gibtown Bike Fest / *Riverview*

Thunder by The Bay Bike Festival / *Sarasota*

Leesburg Bike Fest / *Leesburg*

Daytona Bike Weeks / *Daytona*

Thunder Beach Rally / *Panama City Beach*

High Seas Bike Rally / *Port Canaveral*

Biketoberfest / *Daytona*

St. Pete Bike Fest / *St. Pete Beach*

Daytona Beach which is probably the largest has two bike events a year. The first, which is called *Bike Week* in March lasts two weeks. It has been going on for over 100 years and has had attendance of over 500,000 people for the event in the past. Over the past few year's participation has slowed and currently the number of bikers has dwindled to closer to 200,000 people. They also have a second one called *Biketoberfest* in October that draws another 75,000-125,000 for an official 4-day event.

No matter if you work or are retired, you must always be aware of scammers trying to get your money. Door-to-door salespeople prey on lonely people talking them into buying everything from magazines to home security systems.

Because of an aging population, many with dwindling income and resources, scammers attempt every scheme known to man to take your money. It is common to get four or five phone solicitations daily from people attempting to get your information or sell you something. Now this happens in all states but cheats and scammers target retiree areas such as Florida and Arizona for one major reason, many people let themselves become victims.

It not uncommon to be approached while in a parking lot or at a gas station by a person asking you for money. This even happens while walking on the beach. Everyone has a hard-luck story. **Learn to say NO!**

Some scams that you hear about on television or print are ones that phone you and say you owe a federal or local agency money and if you don't pay immediately you will be arrested. Another popular phone scam is getting a call saying they are your grandchildren and they've been arrested or their lives are in danger so send money fast to save them. Even though that sounds crazy, many people fall for it and give out a credit card number or their social security number and it's over. You've lost your money and possibly your identity.

Almost everywhere in Florida *the tow truck* scam takes place so if you are going to live here or you are a tourist be aware. It works like this. Tow truck companies go to local business' and put's up signs in the parking area saying if you are not using that store you will be towed. This is totally legitimate when the store is open since the parking spaces are for that store, but after hours or weekends when the store is closed and the lot is totally empty, people will park there because of limited parking at popular restaurants, beaches or venues. The tow companies are waiting across the street to tow your vehicle while you are eating or away enjoying your evening.

Most people think that their vehicle has been stolen, but that is rarely what has happened. The tow company has taken it to a compound yard. When you go to get your vehicle there are no police tickets or anything involved, except for the tow company getting as much as they can from you to get your vehicle back. Normally, it takes $200-300 to get it back. If you call the police, they cannot do anything because the sign warned you. The tow company then gives a percentage of the take to the store owner.

I've known two people who have worked for these types of companies and they are paid strictly commission. No tow, no money for them so they are always on the prowl to tow you. **If you see the sign, don't park there.** Being a local doesn't help you, they'll take your money too.

No matter if you work full-time or retired, nosy neighbors are plentiful. People with nothing to do want to know everything you do and if they don't agree with something, you or the HOA will hear about it. It seems that the older you get, the more critical and intolerant of others you get. This is the reality of living in a retirement state.

When I originally moved to Florida from the Midwest, I just brought my personality with me, greeting people, being friendly and did make some friends. After a few years though most of them couldn't make it financially or just got homesick for family and moved back to where they came from. People come and go no matter if it's back to where they started, or end up dying.

For many new Florida residents, being away from family and familiar surroundings becomes a problem. Getting homesick causes many to leave after a few years and return home. For this reason, many local people don't want to get too attached to new friends because they come and go frequently.

Florida cities have some of the highest rates of fatalities for people being hit walking or riding bikes. Over a ten-year period, the state averaged 543 pedestrian deaths a year. A major reason for this is that a lot of people are out walking or riding because of nice weather. In 2019, *Daytona* was ranked the second most pedestrian fatalities of any city in the United States.

With an aging population, seniors have more auto accidents than other age groups. Also, a lot of tourists from all over the world come to Florida and drive. Unfortunately, many are not familiar with the rules-of-the-road in the United States. This is particularly true in the Orlando and Miami regions who have many foreign visitors. Because of these reasons, pedestrian injuries from vehicles are a common occurrence.

To limit your exposure to crowds and not have to pay tourist prices for food and beverage, private clubs are plentiful in Florida to the locals. Civic organizations such as the *Elks, Moose, Eagles* and fraternal ones as the *VFW, American Legion* are in most towns. Members can get cheaper drinks and food, and socialize with people who live in the community.

In the past these organizations had an older, retired membership. The latest trends are that these clubs are attempting to move towards a younger membership. When I say a younger membership, I mean people in their 50's, not there 80's. These organizations also donate time and money to local schools, veterans, meals- on-wheels and other programs in their local communities.

As you see, moving to Florida isn't all *pool-boys* serving you cocktails and fantasy on the veranda. But one thing that you can always do that has always made me feel better no matter if it was a bad day or a good one, is a little bragging telling all my friends and family back home that *"I live in Florida"!*

IT'S ALL ABOUT THE WEATHER

A lthough Florida has lots of water and the activities that surround it, ask any transplant to the state on why they wanted to come here and the answer would be the same, *the weather!*

No matter where people come from to Florida, with maybe the exception of California or Arizona, moving to Florida is a dramatic change in the yearly weather they had experienced in the past. Here are the average high/low temperatures in different Florida cities:

	Jan. Ave. High/Low	July Ave. High/Low
Pensacola	61/43F	89/75F
Jacksonville	66/46F	92/75F
Orlando	72/51F	92/75F
Tampa	71/52F	91/75F
Miami	73/61F	85/71F
Key West	75/65F	90/80F
Gainesville	67/43F	91/72F

On average, Florida has 110+ days per year of 90 degree plus temperatures.

With the state being long geographically, approximately 447 miles from the northern state line to *Key West*, there is only a slight difference in the daily highs and lows. Although Key West is 1,697 miles from the equator, Florida has a tropical atmosphere which makes living here similar to life in a tropical paradise.

Looking on a world map, the country of *Africa* is directly across the Atlantic Ocean from Florida. Most of us relate Africa to hot, tropical climates which it is for the most part. Looking at it this way, Florida would have the same characteristics in weather.

Being such a long state, the northern parts do have colder days, but snow is a true rarity. In fact, snow in Florida has only been documented a few times, with at least forty-years between instances. On those snow days, the high temperatures ended up getting up to 63 degrees during the day, which in some cases resulted in a beach day.

Occasionally a freezing night may occur, but usually around the middle of the state, north of Orlando. *Marion county* which is *Ocala* and northward may get a few freezing temperatures at night but this is limited to a night or two a year.

On a cooler day of 50 degrees, you will see locals dressed up in winter gear, while out-of-state visitors will be in shorts and sandals. Many local residents will tell you that the longer you spend in the heat, the thinner your blood gets resulting in being colder when temperatures go down. The truth being that this is a myth. If you do live in a warm climate and suddenly get cold, it has to do with small surface blood vessels that take longer to dilate and you may feel a chill, but nothing to do with thinner blood.

From personal experience after moving back north to a cold weather area in winter, after twelve years in Florida, the winters didn't bother me at all. In fact, after experiencing warm weather and going back to cold weather I felt more comfortable in the cold.

Many people who do return back to northern locales after living in Florida, will say that they moved back because of the humidity and the oppressive heat of the summer. Yes, the average temperature in summer is a few degrees higher than most states north but the humidity according to the *National Weather Service* is no different than that of *New York City*, *St Louis* or *Dallas* during summer months.

In Florida, there is a definite difference in the heat on your body and skin depending on where you live within the state. If you live within about fifteen miles of a coastline, you generally can get a nice breeze throughout the year which helps keep you a little cooler. Temperatures near the coastlines also are normally a few degrees lower and a lower heat-index than inland towns.

Living in interior regions without that breeze can mean it feels hotter since mother-nature's breezes aren't helping to keep you cool.

Weather can have a large influence on how crowded the area where you live is going to be. In the winter months, particularly from Christmas to April, snowbirds flock to the state to get away from the northern United States and Canadian winters. Snowbirds are people who move to Florida yearly for two to four months escaping cold weather. You may also consider it like an extended vacation. In some areas, they can double the local population which makes daily living such as driving, golfing, the grocery store and eating out much more time consuming because of being busier.

In the spring, besides having the snowbirds, coastal areas have an influx of spring breakers usually during the month of March and early April. The makeup for these spring breakers varies from area to area. Some cities promote having college and high school age people while others cater more to families. Needless to say, there is a major difference in the experience you will have living in Florida depending on the type of spring breaker you get.

The spring also brings many large festivals, fairs and events to Florida which effects daily life in some areas because of tourist.

Larger ones include the *Daytona 500* and *Bike Week in Daytona*; *Emerald Coast Cruisin Car Show, Thunder Beach Motorcycle Rally* and *The Seabreeze Jazz Festival* in *Panama City; Carnival Miami* and *Miami Open Tennis Championships, Mardi Gras at Busch Garden in Tampa and Major League Baseball spring training.* Almost all cities have multiple winter and spring line-ups of events.

The summer months brings the vacationers which Florida is known for. In 2019, the state boasted that it had 131 million vacationers visit the state. The coastlines and Orlando get the majority of these visitors. Orlando alone had 75 million visitors in 2018. That makes Orlando the #1 tourist destination in the United States. Compare that to the 42 million who visited Las Vegas that same year. *Disney, Universal Studios, Sea World, Gatorland and Legoland* are just a few of the major attractions in the Orlando area.

The warm tropical weather of Florida is nice but it also has some negatives. Burnt, premature aging to the skin are everyday problems in the Floridian lifestyle. After a few years of enjoying the sun, many Floridians avoid going out into it. Florida has the highest percentage of population that gets skin cancer in the United States at 7.1% of its population.

Though the word cancer is scary, skin cancer is one of the easiest to prevent and when diagnosed properly is fairly easy to resolve. Everyday Floridians just live with the thought that it might happen to them one day and will deal with it accordingly.

Daily life alone exposes you to the relentless sun and though you cover your skin, arms, ears, necks, face and top of the head which are common areas of skin cancer, the sun still gets you. Over years of exposure problems, premature aging and skin cancers occurs.

I personally have experienced skin cancer five times while being in Florida. Skin cancer develops over a lifetime, so just moving here doesn't trigger it. If you have exposure in younger years to the sun then chances increase you will have a problem later in life. The intense sun in Florida can increase your chances of having a problem with your skin.

If you are worried about skin issues, then use a lot of sunscreen and blockers always, wear UV resistant clothing, put a hat on your head with a wider brim and stay indoors during the intense sun hours during the day. If all of this fails, there are an overabundance of dermatologists available ready to scrape and remove skin problems.

Weather also triggers other events such as hurricanes and tropical storms. In the summer when the oceans heat up, weather systems develop on the coast of *Africa* before heading west across the Atlantic Ocean. Some of these tropical depressions gain strength and not only effect Florida, but also the Caribbean islands, Mexican coastline, southern United States coastline in the Gulf of Mexico and eastern United States coastline in the Atlantic Ocean.

Hurricane season starts June 1st and continues through November 30th. The state is pretty resilient when it comes to damage from these storms. When one hits and possibly wipes out major areas or cities, rebuilding comes fast. Hurricanes are just a part of living the Florida lifestyle.

The forecast of a hurricane and preparation in your area is a major inconvenience to say the least. Normally, near the coast line the weather service and state officials will require an evacuation. Although the winds can be vicious and destroy everything in sight, most damage and deaths occur from flooding.

When evacuation orders are given, many people stay and try to survive the wrath of the storm, but that is usually pretty stupid on their part. These people not only put their own lives in jeopardy, but also the emergency services that will have to save them later.

If a hurricane does hit, not everyone is required to evacuate, but will still be affected by the storm. Before the storm, stores will be sold out of all liquids, generators, canned food items, charcoal, etc. ATM's will be empty, so cash won't be available, sometimes for a week. Gasoline lines may take hours to be rationed a limited number of gallons for your vehicle or generator. Eventually, there will be no gasoline available.

When the storm hits, you may suffer without no electricity for up to two weeks. Your refrigerator will eventually heat up and everything will perish in it. With no electricity, cell phone service, etc. you will be isolated. You cannot use water from your faucet since municipal water supplies will be contaminated. Power lines and trees will be scattered on the roads and your local governments will have state-of-emergency orders that you cannot be out running around.

Hurricanes hit in summer months so it's also hot outside. Without air conditioning, a fan, cold drinks you'll find that each hour drags your attitude and physical capability lower and lower. People who have health issues, these storms could be a difference between life and death. After days or weeks of this, you will be short on patience and on the edge of exploding.

But as I had said earlier, the state knows how to survive and recover from these types of catastrophes. In many countries, a hurricane will affect lives for months or years, in Florida it's days or weeks.

During one hurricane in 2004, I evacuated to *Biloxi, Mississippi* which was nine hours from my home. We had ourselves and two cats. Found a small hotel on the Gulf of Mexico who let our animals stay so that was good. We had planned on staying five or six days and return home. After two weeks we finally got information that electricity was back on and it was safe to return.

It took almost twenty hours to get back home because besides us, another 3 million people were trying to do the same thing, return home. Interstates poked along at 15 miles per hour, fender benders were three per mile, cars running out of gas lined the highways, gas stations on every exit were closed. Most people would never realize any of these things unless experiencing them personally.

If you have damage at your residence, you will have to find temporary ways to patch it up. Broken windows can be boarded, roof leaks can be tarped. An army of roofers and contractors usually flock to hurricane ravished areas since work and potential insurance money is plentiful. But beware, a normal $9,000 roof job will now cost $25,000 if you want it done immediately. Prices are gouged and inflated due to the disaster.

In an ironic twist of fate, *Hurricane Katrina* which hit Louisiana, Mississippi and Alabama in August 2005, washed away into the Gulf of Mexico the motel I had evacuated to in Biloxi, MS while escaping the Florida hurricane the previous year.

According to *Wikipedia*, more hurricanes hit Florida than any other state. Although this sounds very intimidating, since the year 2000, only 7 major hurricanes has struck Florida. Major hurricanes are ones that are rated *category 3, 4* or *5* with sustained winds of 111 mph -158 mph plus.

Since the year 2010, only two major hurricanes have hit Florida. These two were *Irma* in 2017 and *Michael* in 2018.

Thunderstorms that include lightening are common. Florida is known as '*The Lightening Capital of the World*'! According to *Accuweather.com*, a ten-year study showed that there were 1.2 million lightning strikes in the state of Florida per year. That's about 3,500 per day! *Central Florida* is also known as *Lightening Alley*. From Tampa on the west coast, through Orlando, to Titusville on the east coast, lightening is a common occurrence. A *Florida State University* study found that lightening kills about ten people per year in the state.

Going back to the theme in the beginning of this chapter, most people move to Florida for the weather. That's a very good reason to come and enjoy making it your paradise. But as you can see, even in paradise, you may not experience a snowstorm, but other related problems replace these as potential weather issues.

THE COST-OF-LIVING

According to the *World Population Review*, results taken in 2020, the state of Florida ranks 25th in overall cost-of-living of the fifty-states. In this report, Florida's *Cost-Index is 97.9.* Below are the twenty-four states and their *Cost-Index* that rank ahead of Florida:

Hawaii 192.9	California 151.7	New York 139.1
Oregon 134.2	Massachusetts 131.6	Alaska 129.9
Maryland 129.7	Connecticut 127.7	New Jersey 125.1
Rhode Island 119.4	Maine 117.5	Vermont 114.5
Washington 110.7	New Hampshire 109.7	Nevada 108.5
Delaware 108.1	Montana 106.9	Colorado 105.6
Pennsylvania 101.7	Minnesota 101.6	Virginia 100.7
South Dakota 100.7	North Dakota 98.8	Utah 98.4

If you are moving from one of the above states then you may be able to get more bang-for-your-dollar than where your last home was. Beware though that this can be a little deceiving, living costs will be higher in some regions of Florida than others.

You can relate this to your current home state. If you live in *New York*, then the area around *New York City* would be much more expensive than living in the central part of the state. Areas that are in more demand because of jobs, social life, water recreation, etc. will raise the cost-of-living in that area to be higher than if you live in a rural area.

Now if you relocate from a state that isn't on the list above, then your overall cost-of-living may the higher when moving to the *Sunshine State*, and in some cases quite a bit higher. Without listing all the states that have a lower cost-of-living than Florida, here are twelve states with a lower *Cost-Index:*

Mississippi 86.1	Arkansas 86.9	Oklahoma 87.0	Missouri 87.1
New Mexico 87.5	Tennessee 88.7	Michigan 88.9	Kansas 89.0
Georgia 89.2	Wyoming 89.3	Alabama 89.3	Indiana 90.0

If you are moving from a state with higher a cost-of-living, then you will be happy moving to Florida. If you are moving from a state with a lower overall cost-of-living, then of course you may be in for a big change.

Although Florida may seem overall reasonable on the cost-of-living compared to the rest of the country, some areas of the state are more expensive to live in than others. Using data from the website *Salary.com,* let's look at some of the regions of Florida and the cost-of-living compared to other United States cities.

The following is derived by using the *Consumer Price Index (CPI)* of 300+ U.S. cities for comparison to Florida cities against the national average:

Panhandle

Pensacola *-11.8%*	Destin *-12.4%*	Panama City *-13.3%*

West Coast

Clearwater *-5.4%*	St. Petersburg *-5.5%*	Clearwater *-5.4%*
Sarasota *+3.3%*	Port Charlotte *-1.3%*	Fort Myers *-3.2%*

Spring Hill *-6.2%*   Marco Island *-3.2%*   Naples *-3.8%*

The Keys

Key Largo *+7.0%*   Marathon *+7.0%*   Key West *+7.2%*

East Coast

Miami *+11.6%*	Ft Lauderdale *+11.4%*	Delray Beach *+10.5%*
Port St Lucie *+1.5%*	Vero Beach *-6.9%*	New Smyrna Bch *-7.1%*
Cocoa Beach *-6.6%*	Palm Bay *-6.9%*	Daytona Bch *-7.0%*
St Augustine *-7.8%*	Hollywood *+11.4%*	Orange Park *-7.5%*
Palm Beach *+10.2%*	Melbourne *-6.3%*	Palm Coast *-7.6%*
Jacksonville *-7.4%*	Boca Raton *+10.5%*	Fernandina Bch *-8.0%*

Central (Inland)

Lake City *-7.2%*	Gainesville *-6.6%*	Ocala *-7.2%*
Orlando *-0.8%*	Kissimmee *-1.1%*	Lakeland *-6.2%*
The Villages *-1.4%*	Sebring *-3.5%*	Winter Garden *-0.9%*

If you would like to compare the cost-of-living of your current home to any city in Florida, good, accurate information is available on *www.Salary.com*! Here you can get an unbiased comparison that may assist you in what potential living costs are for the area's you are considering relocation to.

On the quality of your life, in regards to having money to spend depends on if you are retiring with a substantial amount of money in the bank and possibly a pension, if you are going to rely on social security for the bulk of your income or if you are planning to work and make a living based strictly on your current income.

Keep in mind from a previous chapter on *Jobs, Work & Income*, the wage scale in Florida is below many states and the average household income is less than thirty-two other states (includes D.C). This is one of the major reasons people moving to Florida find themselves working more, not enjoying the activities they moved here for, and end up moving back to higher-paying jobs from areas they had previously came from.

Utility costs are very reasonable. Electric is advertised as one of the lowest rates in the United States. Though you use very little electricity for a furnace in winter months, you do use it to cool yourself down up to nine-months a year. This makes up for the amount you save from heating with a furnace.

The cost of recreation is fairly reasonable in Florida. A golfer has an unlimited number of courses throughout the state and can play 365 days a year. Cost of a round with cart can be as low as $12 in non-peak times. Golfing is more expensive during the winter months when snowbirds are here enjoying a round during their stays.

Florida residents are normally offered major discounts or yearly passes at most theme parks that makes it affordable to go multiple times a year. These discounts usually apply to admission and possibly parking, not food, drinks and other special activities inside the parks.

Automobile insurance rates are much more expensive than most other states. Two recent surveys in early 2019 has shown that

Florida has the third highest automobile insurance rates in the United States. The highest in the United States is Michigan.

According to *StudyAtInsure.com*, a consumer insurance website, Florida is among a handful of states with a *no-fault* auto insurance system. With the *no-fault* insurance a driver must also carry medical coverage on their auto insurance to cover their own injuries regardless of who is at fault in an accident. Legally a driver must carry this additional insurance no matter how much coverage they already have from personal health plans or Medicare. This is called *personal injury protection* or *PIP*.

PIP raises premiums dramatically and in over fifty percent of situations is not needed since the buyer has other medical insurances, but required to purchase it to stay legal.

As an example of the cost we are talking, moving from the state of Illinois, my premium was $530/year full-coverage. In Florida with the same limits and company, my premium went up to $910/year.

The same is true for motorcycle coverage. In Illinois I paid less than $300/ year to Florida at $850/year.

If you have multiple vehicles this additional cost could be a major burden if you are living on a tight budget.

Another problem with automobile insurance is since the cost is so high, many drivers have no insurance or only carry the minimums. Twenty-six percent of Florida's drivers fall into the no insurance or minimal category. That's 1 in 4 drivers with none or inadequate auto insurance.

In 2017-2018 the Florida legislature took up the debate on getting costs lower, but lobbying from insurance company interests stopped potential legislation that would reduce costs. In 2019, the legislature debated again in an attempt to bring auto insurance costs down. It failed once again.

Once you move to Florida and establish a permanent residence, you have 30 days to surrender your previous state' license and get a Florida license. Part-time residents can obtain a Florida driver license but must surrender their previous state's license. You cannot hold multiple licenses from different states.

Regular Florida license plates with the *orange* (fruit) in the center of the plate comes with either the slogan *The Sunshine State* or with the *county you live in*. It is your choice; no extra cost is involved. You can also purchase one of 135 designer plates that help fund various organizations. The cost of this type of plate is $25/year extra.

The majority of my adult life I have worked in the automobile industry as a manager at car dealerships. I've held almost every job in the dealership on the sales end so I consider myself knowledgeable about the industry and in purchasing a vehicle. If you plan on purchasing a new or used vehicle in the future, check out these on the *Money Pro Series*, '*Save Thousands on Your Next New Vehicle*', and '*Save Thousands on Your Next Used Vehicle*'.

Consumer protection laws for buying a vehicle in Florida are laxed compared to many other states. Dealers definitely take advantage of these areas when it comes to making money off you when purchasing a vehicle or motorcycle.

In most states, dealers are allowed to put onto the contract, which is usually not included in your negotiation, the sales tax, license, title fees and a *documentary fee* or *DOC fee*. This DOC fee is supposedly the cost of doing the paperwork and normally is regulated by the state. DOC fees can be under $100 to about $250.

In Florida, dealer's also charge the DOC fee, but also add a *Dealer Fee* on new or used vehicles. On top of that they have recently started charging a *Reconditioning fee* on used vehicles besides all the other fees.

These fees are not only on cars and trucks but also for motorcycles. Most dealer fees are upward of $1000, while some who also charge reconditioning fees on a used vehicle are an additional $1000. None of these are disclosed to the consumer until they get into the finance office after hours of test-driving, negotiation, etc. Normally, the consumer is so worn down by this point or too embarrassed to argue, just agree to them and end up paying up to $2000-3000 too much!

If you plan on purchasing vehicles after your move to Florida these fees can substantially raise the cost of the vehicle. If you plan on adding a vehicle, consider buying before moving.

The cost of opening a business in Florida is in line with most other areas of the country. Rent rates, start-up fees, licenses, etc. are in line with most other cities and states.

One big difference in opening a business is that you can operate one out of your home in most areas of the state. I've experienced several times in the past in the Midwest, that wouldn't allow the operation of a legal business out of a home, no matter if it was a part-time or internet one.

In Florida, a home business doesn't seem to be much of a problem to have. Get on *Google maps* and when pulling up an area, you will see private homes with a business using that address. I've known several people who do this from motorcycle repair, to food catering, to home cleaning to internet sales performing their business from home.

Many Homeowner's Associations (HOA) in Florida don't allow for a business to be ran from a private home. If you do plan on operating a business from home then be sure that the rules and regulations of the neighborhood allow it.

Many newcomers to Florida who have successful business' from where they came from, attempt to open a new one here. After living here a couple of years, you will start seeing them open and fail within a year or two. The only thing I can surmise from this is that sales were not what was expected because of lower incomes and not targeting tourist who would spend more money than locals.

If you had a successful business in the past and plan on opening one in Florida, be sure to research and plan ahead. A successful one from your past doesn't guarantee success here.

Florida does allow you to save money!!! Each year they have a tax holiday when purchasing hurricane supplies and school supplies. Unfortunately, these savings don't amount to more than a few dollars, but they are a savings!

I had pointed this out earlier, but want to repeat it, if you are retiring full-time or plan on part-time work you will have lots of free time on your hands. It can get expensive doing nothing all day. After so much sitting around and watching television, cutting the grass, etc. you'll find yourself going out eating, drinking, etc. which all adds up day after day.

Although this shouldn't be considered a cost-of-living, it is additional money coming out of your pocket to live. Be aware of these unforeseen financial consequences of retirement!

RETIRING IN FLORIDA

Though most of the thoughts in this chapter are ones that I've touched on throughout this book, I wanted to dedicate these pages to only people planning on living their retirement years in Florida.

After a lifetime of hard work, being able to move to paradise is like making a dream come true. After talking to hundreds of people over the years, moving to Florida is probably the number one goal the majority had after years of living in cold weather. If you are one of those people, your dream can come true, but be sure that you know the challenge ahead of you.

According to *Wallethub*, Florida is considered the best state to retire in for several reasons. Items such as no personal income tax, no estate taxes, no intangible taxes on vehicles, etc. enhances the reasons why people want to live in Florida.

First, be sure you know where you may want to live. Internet research has made this much easier than in the past. Websites such as *CityData.com* can give you valuable information about any town you're considering. It will give you average housing costs, crime statistics, population stats, cost-of-living, etc.

Salary.com will give you cost-of-living data comparison from your current hometown to any potential city you are considering to move to. If you plan on working after your move, you can also obtain salary comparisons.

Reading an areas online newspaper, will also give you valuable information about the region and things happening there. Find the newspaper in the cities of your potential move and get an online subscription for a few months. You will learn what goes on locally from day-to-day. After reading a cities daily news you may find out that it's not an area you would want to live.

A popular, ever-growing retirement area forty-five miles north of Orlando is a development called *The Villages*. In the 1970's and 80's, this area started as a mobile home community but has since grown into a 32 square mile region with homes and condos along with mobile homes.

Sumter County is the home of *The Villages* with portions entering *Lake* and *Marion Counties*. The *US Census* in 2013-2014 stated that this area was the *fastest growing city in America*. Also, from 2010-2017 it was the *fastest growing metropolitan area of the country*.

The Villages is made up of seventeen *Community Development Districts* governed by an elected board of residents. All but three of these districts are limited to age restrictions. The three that are not are for families of younger ages.

Within *The Villages*, golfing, recreational activities, healthcare, commercial shopping and a total self-contained retirement lifestyle is available.

In 2017, *Forbes* magazine named *The Villages* to the list of *The 25 Best Places to Retire in the United States* for the second time! Besides this, *The Villages* has received dozens of other accolades over the years.

A documentary that is available on life in *The Villages* has been produced called, *'Some Kind of Heaven'*. If you are considering moving to this area, check out the documentary to get insights on how life is there.

There are many planned communities for retirees throughout the state of Florida, *The Villages* is the biggest and most famous.

Some other Retirement communities in Florida has developed into great places to live an active lifestyle include:

On Top of The World Communities: *Ocala*

Cyprus Lakes 55+ Community: *Lakeland*

Margaritaville: *Daytona Beach*

Buttonwood Village: *Punta Gorda*

Hyde Park 55+ Community: *Winter Garden*

Arlington Ridge: *Leesburg*

These are only a few of the communities established for retirees or mature people. Needless to say, chances are that there is a similar community in about every county in the state. A little internet research can assist you in finding one in your potential new home area.

After you have narrowed down your search to a few areas, vacation or take a short trip there. Each area will have a different flavor of fun and excitement. Be sure that you've experienced it before making your move.

From past experience, I thought that certain cities were going to be my dream come true, but after researching them, reading the local news and visiting them, I realized that they didn't have things that I really wanted in my personal paradise. If I would have blindly moved to that area, a lot of money would have been wasted making the move, and I would not have been happy. If I had made a wrong move, I would have been financially devastated moving again to another location.

After finding the city you want to live your retirement in, you must next decide to either rent or purchase. If renting, again the local newspaper will be helpful. National websites such as *apartment.com* can also be a great help giving you all price ranges of living quarters and the amenities they have to offer!

If you decide to purchase, contact a local realtor in that area and let them work for you. This is very common in Florida. Realtors do the majority of their business long-distance assisting people who plan on moving to Florida full-time or to purchase second homes.

Also, some self-research using websites like *Zillow.com* or *Realtor.com* will list almost all the available homes, condos, multi-family and mobile homes for sale in that area. You can also see what previously sold homes has gone for.

If purchasing, you have many options. A single-family home, condominium, multi-family unit or mobile home all have their advantages and disadvantages. Much depends on your future needs and how much money you have to spend.

Most people when retiring to Florida end up down-sizing from their current lifestyle. Two-bedroom homes are abundant here to accommodate those downsizing. When thinking about how large of a dwelling you plan on moving to, keep in mind that after you move to Florida, you'll have family and friends that will surely be visiting and staying with you.

If you purchase a home instead of renting, be sure to ask your realtor about applying for your *homestead extension* if you live here full-time. This is done through your local *county tax appraiser*. Your realtor or closing agent will have all the details.

As a full-time retiree you will probably stay very busy as you enjoy all the new surroundings of your community and what the area has to offer!

Many newcomers find that getting a part-time job not only keeps them busy, and their mind active, but also some extra income is nice. This will also allow for you to meet people in your local area that can get you up-to-speed on what's happening in your new hometown.

Cheap golf, fraternal organizations such as the *Elks, Eagles, VFW, Moose,* and *American Legion* are all places to socialize and have good times. Local towns and cities also have clubs and town organizations for seniors that meet multiple times a week playing cards, having meals, playing horseshoes, pickle ball, golf, bowling leagues, and bingo plus a variety of activities that is inexpensive or free.

One of the major reasons people leave Florida after a few years is that they become homesick from where they came. The children, grandkids, friends, etc. are missed. This is why it's important to have them come visit, plus stay active, which includes working at a job or volunteer work so these emotions won't set in.

Some warnings for the retiree are beware of scammers. Door-to-door sales and telemarketers are everywhere. If a proposal seems too good to be true, it probably is a scam. If you are solicited for money and you didn't originally engage the solicitation, it's definitely a scam. This happens hundreds of times a day in Florida. Don't be victimized.

Most retirees who move to Florida have thought of moving here for years before they actually do it. If you fall into that category just don't think about it, do your homework and research while waiting to make your move. Doing that, will make the move much easier and much more enjoyable once you get here!

BECOMING A SNOWBIRD

Many people who are just tired of living out the winter months in cold weather areas, but also don't want to pack up everything and permanently move, ends up becoming **snowbirds**!

Snowbirds come to Florida from one to four months, normally during the winter. This has been a tradition for people since the early 1900's when many wealthy people from the Northeast United States found great pleasure in building 2nd homes in Florida. Becoming a snowbird allows for you to enjoy the best of both worlds, summer at home and winter in Florida.

Some winter visitors bring their own motor homes, or travel-trailers to stay at one of the many campgrounds or state parks throughout the state. More common though, are visitors who lease or rent a home, apartment, condo, timeshare or hotel room for the months they visit. There is an abundance of availability once you start looking.

Websites such as *VRBO, Craigslist, FloridaForBoomers.com, FloridaSnowbird.com* and *VacationRentals.com* will get you in contact with owners looking to rent out their property.

The cost for winter accommodations for a month or more range from $900-3000 per month. Of course, you can pay more for bigger and better places but for most around $1,300-1,500 is common.

Bringing your own vehicle is the best way to go. Renting a car for months at a time can really add to the overall cost. Also, driving here allows for you to bring a car full of comfort items and clothing. Flying would cost a fortune in extra bags.

Most accommodations that cater to snowbirds include some type of kitchen or kitchenette so you can make meals if you desire. Also, most have some type of laundry facility or access to one. They also provide cookware, glassware, coffee pots, toasters, dinnerware and linen. Other than your clothing, most provide everything.

Many snowbirds belong to fraternal organizations in their home towns such as the *Elks, VFW, American Legion, Moose* and *Eagles*. As members already, they are allowed to visit and use the local clubs in Florida. Some of these organizations also allows out-of-state members to park their motorhomes at the club for a donation while visiting the area.

After being a snowbird, many decide on making the permanent change and move to Florida. If you have a desire to move here, then becoming a snowbird for a few winters to make sure that moving here would be the right move for you is a great idea. It's a lot less expensive visiting for a couple of years, for a few months, than selling everything, packing up and moving here permanently then regretting the move.

Besides Florida being a major destination for snowbirds, Arizona has also become known for their winter guests also. The majority of snowbirds in Florida are from the Northeast, Midwest, Eastern Canada and Europe.

If you bring pets as a snowbird the challenge may be a little greater. Although you will be welcomed with open arms, there is a limited number of living facilities that allow pets for prolonged stays. Don't get me wrong, they are available, but it may take a little more effort on your part to find them and make the arrangements.

If you plan on being a snowbird, planning well ahead would be best. Many accommodations get reserved a year ahead of time.

Waiting until the last month or final weeks before you arrive will cut down on your options of what's available.

Many snowbirds will come year after year to the same accommodation. Friendships and lifetime memories can be made doing this. Again, this is a great way to see if the Florida lifestyle is for you.

If you're planning to become a first-time snowbird or trying a different city than your past trips, go online and read the local newspaper a few months before you leave home. This will get you up-to-speed before you arrive knowing about what's happening in the area in regards to activities, concerts, events, etc.

Even loose-planning of your trip prior to it will allow for you to take full advantage of what that area has to offer.

Don't be shy when you arrive in your winter home, you will be welcomed with open-arms. The locals love having you!

COSTS OF MOVING TO FLORIDA

I f you have ever moved across town then you know moving isn't much fun. The anxiety and stress are bad enough, but then filtering in the costs involved can make you go nuts! If you have lived in your current home for twenty or thirty years then you can imagine moving a lifetime of stuff. Well, moving 500 miles or 2,000 on top of that can get very expensive and stressful.

Below is a check list and estimated costs involved of making an interstate move. I've tried to put down several scenarios with a range of costs involved. Other than using the estimates of moving, you can use the chart to keep track of your actual spending when it occurs.

This list includes items that will financially cost you money. Not listed are things such as changing your postal address, bank accounts, disconnecting current utilities, etc, since those are free or low-cost things you must do before or during the move.

The **Pre-Move** are costs you will incur before the move as you research the area you may want to live. Costs will vary but your actual cost should fall within the *Estimated Cost* guidelines given. Some *Functions* listed may be avoided or not needed which will result in a zero-cost to you.

(Pre-Move)

Function	Estimated Cost	Your Estimate	Actual Cost
Local Newspapers/Research	$10-20/month		
Vacations/Trips	$800-$1500 ea.		

Storage Unit	$100–200/month		
Cleaning Costs	$20–$150		

Cost of The Move will vary depending on if you hire a professional mover or if you do everything yourself. Also, the final costs will vary on the distance of the move. If you are moving 300 miles, that would be much less than moving 1500 miles.

(The Move)

Function	Estimated Cost	Your Estimate	Actual Cost
Moving Company	$5500–12000		
Rental Truck	$800–2000		
Labor/Help	$25 hr/person		
Tolls	$0–50		
Moving Supplies, boxes, dollies, etc.	$50–250		
Rental Truck Insurance	$45–150		
Pet Transportation	$0–300		
Storage (if needed)	$100–200/month		
Lodging	$85–200/night		
Rental Truck Fuel	$375/1k mile		
Food	$20/day/person		

If you plan on renting when you move, the costs incurred would be less than if you purchased immediately, although, these costs can be substantial. The following table are *Functions* and *Estimated Costs* for renting.

(Renting)

Function	Estimated Cost	Your Estimate	Actual Cost
Storage (if needed)	$100–200/month		
Rental Deposit	$1000–2500		
Utility Deposit	$100–350		
Auto Registration	$200–300/vehicle		
TV/Internet Deposit	$75–200		
Renters Insurance	$150–350/year		
Food/Household Supplies	$200–600		
School Fees/Supplies	$50–200/child		
Hurricane Kit Supplies	$200–3500		
Home Furnishings	$0–5000		
Cleaning Supplies	$25–150		
Hired Cleaner	$20–$30/hr		

The following chart includes costs of purchasing a home or condo. Again, the dollar amounts are estimates only. You may not incur all the items listed.

(Home/Condo Purchase)

Function	Estimated Cost	Your Estimate	Actual Cost
Storage (if needed)	$100–200/month		
Home Inspection	$125–450		
Land Survey	$75–300		
Termite Inspection	$0–125		
Roof/Wind Mitigation Inspection	$75–200		
Escrow/Down Payment	0–20% of home purchase price		
Closing Costs	2–5% of purchase price		
Utility Deposits	$100–350		
TV/Internet Deposit	$75–200		
Paint/Locks/Rehab	$75–5000		
Homeowners Insurance	$1500–4000		
Cleaning Supplies	$25–150		
Auto Registration	$200–300/vehicle		

Food/Household Supplies	$200-600		
School Fees/Supplies	$50-200/child		
Hurricane Kit Supplies	$200-3500		
Home Furnishings	$0-5000		
HOA Dues/Fees	$0-4800		

The following chart includes costs of purchasing a mobile home. Again, the dollar amounts are estimates only. You may not incur all the items listed.

(Mobile Home Purchase)

Function	Estimated Cost	Your Estimate	Actual Cost
Storage (if needed)	$100-200/month		
Home Inspection	$125-400		
Termite Inspection	$0-125		
Escrow/Down Payment	20-30% of purchase price		
Closing Costs	2-5% of purchase price		
Utility Deposits	$100-350		
TV/Internet Deposit	$75-200		
Background Check Fee	$35-125/person		
Paint/Locks/Rehab	$75-5000		

Homeowners Insurance	$600–2000		
Cleaning Supplies	$25–150		
Hired Cleaner	$25–30/hr/person		
Auto Registration	$275–300/vehicle		
Food/Household Supplies	$200–600		
School Fees/Supplies	$50–200/child		
Hurricane Kit Supplies	$200–3500		
Park Fees	$350–900/month		
Home Furnishings	$0–5000		

When determining the cost of your move don't be too conservative. Often people don't take into consideration all the costs involved of moving, then they find that they are higher than originally planned for or expected.

If you plan on using a professional mover, be aware that not all companies are ethical or transparent. Check with your local *Better Business Bureau (BBB)* and also *Google* search the company for complaints and reviews. You can also contact the *American Moving and Storage Association* for local movers that they recommend.

Because of the intense competition between professional moving companies, many times they will *low-ball* the price to get your business, then will nickel-and-dime you driving up the total cost. This industry has minimal regulations so it's up to the company itself to be fair and honest.

When you get estimates from the mover, you must be willing to ask them lots of questions so that you won't become a victim or your household items won't end up being held hostage until you pay huge extra fees. Here is a list of items that you should ask the company before making your decision:

-Additional charge for labor and supplies? How much?

-Is moving insurance for your possessions supplied or offered?

-Is there a fee for assembly of furniture?

-Is there a bulky item surcharge? *ie: piano, lawn mower, etc.*

-Is there an elevator fee to go beyond the ground floor?

-Is there a long carry fee? If so, how much?

-Is there a cancellation fee? *This can be from $50-300.*

-If your new home is delayed, what's the storage fee?

-Is there an express delivery fee?

-What is the travel fee?

-Is there a hoisting fee? *Door frames may be too small.*

-Is there an environmental charge or disposal fee?

Tipping the movers is common on top of the price you pay. Generally, the foreman should be tipped $50-100, while each laborer would be $20-40. The more complicated the move, the better the tip.

If you make the move yourself, you may have to hire some labor to assist you. If this is the case then count on about $25/hour for each helper. Tipping here is up to you.

Moving isn't easy, and if you are doing it cross-country it can be downright difficult and expensive as you can see. Approach your move smart by doing your homework. Approaching it this way may save you thousands of dollars!

As a conclusion, I want to encourage you to make your dreams a reality. If your dream is to move to Florida then start preparing now, no matter if you plan on an immediate move or waiting a few years. Preparation will make the move easier and you can start enjoying the *Florida lifestyle* as soon as you get here!

See you at the beach!!!!